Murals

Sally Cowan

Contents

Murals

Murals are big pictures.
They are put
in lots of places.

They can be inside **buildings** and outside buildings.

3

Making Murals

Murals are put onto fences, walls, or sidewalks.

Some murals are painted onto big sheets of paper or cardboard.

Some murals are made from lots of little **tiles**.

The tiles are glued onto the wall to make a picture.

Big murals can take a long time to make.

Murals in Schools

Lots of schools have murals. The children and teachers make them.

Some families come to school to help.

Beautiful Murals

Lots of murals

are very beautiful.

Old walls can look better if murals are painted on them.

What Murals Do

Murals can show us places we have not seen before, like the forest or the sea.

Murals can tell a story, too.

Lots of Murals

We can see murals all around the **world**.

Glossary

buildings

tiles

world